Hello! My name is Money.

A BLIND DATE WITH MONEY

OLUBUNMI SAMUEL-ADEYEMI

HELLO! MY NAME IS MONEY.

── Olubunmi Samuel-Adeyemi ──

Dedication

Oluwaseun Fawunmi was used mightily of God to teach and model the principles I have captured here.

Thank you, dear Daddy, for living according to the principles for wealth management.

Thank you, too, for encouraging me to try them out - even promising as I practiced cautiously all those years, to bankroll any challenges I come into in the course of testing these principles.

Because of you, millions around the world now have an opportunity at improved standards of living and wealth perpetuation.

At the time of going to press,
every possible effort has been made to ensure that the information in
this book is accurate, yet does not constitute professional advice.
Accordingly, the author, the publisher and agents shall not accept any
responsibility for loss or damage occasioned to anyone acting, or
refraining from acting as a result of the information in this publication.

ISBN: 978-978-962-745-5
Published in Nigeria by Media DNA
20, Safaratu Sekoni Street, Gbagada, Lagos, Nigeria
books@mediadna.com.ng
+2348054259757

Introduction

Hello, there! My name is Money.
What's your name?

....
(Please enter your full name here)

It's my pleasure to finally sit down with you.
How are you?
And, how are your finances doing?
Great?
Not so great and could be better?

Or, is this such an uncomfortable topic for you, you'd rather not think about it, let alone talk about it?

Tough though it might be for you, I'd like us to spend some time thinking through a few things together. I am certain that this discussion was meant to hold at some point in your life and could well be today.

Again, I am optimistic that this conversation is about to change the course of your life. It will impact not just you, but many generations of those who may come to this world through you.

The conversation we are about to have will be a reference point in your life, definitely making it into your autobiography (yes, your life will be so spectacular, you will have to write one).

So, let's delve in. Shall we?

Page

Dedication   3

Introduction   5

CHAPTER ONE   I Am...   8

CHAPTER TWO   I Am Not...   13

CHAPTER THREE   My Attributes   19

CHAPTER FOUR   How To Engage With Me...   26

CHAPTER FIVE   Now That You Know...   33

About LIMER Personal Finance   40

About the Book   41

About the Author   42

Acknowledgments   43

CHAPTER
ONE

I Am...

I was born way before 650 B.C when the first metal coins were minted in the kingdom of Lydia (in Asia minor). At that time, interactions around the world were mainly by the exchange of goods and services. Being a predominantly agrarian economy, each person went to his farm each day to cultivate crops - all kinds of crops. Then at harvest time, everyone visits the market place to exchange his own farm produce for something else he needs.

So Human A, for example, comes with oranges to be exchanged for tubers of Yam. As soon as he is able to achieve that, he heads home to rest ahead of the next day's harvest.

Let's say the next day he shows up in the market again. Human A will likely come along with oranges again, but probably need Beans this time (not Yam like the day before). So, Human A goes in search of another human who has beans and needs oranges.

Well, what are the odds that such a human being exists? When he finds a person (say Human B) who has the beans he needs, but does not want the oranges he has to offer, he has to stick with that person until he finds another human (let's call this person Human C) who has the tomatoes that Human B needs and wants his (Human A's) oranges.

In essence, Human A gives oranges to Human C, receives tomatoes from him and presents the tomatoes to Human B who has the beans he needs and needs tomatoes in exchange.

But what happens if Human C wants corn and not oranges as possessed by Human A? The need will arise for a Human D who has corn and wants oranges for the corn.

You can begin to imagine how cumbersome the process of trade must have been at the time. Can you picture a string of 10 people at the market with neither possessing what the other needs and everyone needing an 11th person to make the exchange possible?

Well, I was born in the midst of this chaos!

My birth was very strategic. With time, there were so many other problems I came to solve for humans. But, at the beginning, my immediate responsibility was to facilitate trade. As you may have guessed, I was not born like humans are. I did not have a father who had sex with my mother and got carried in her womb for 9 months before coming to the world. I did not have a naming ceremony after 8 days, did not suck for 2 years then gradually get weaned and resume elementary school.

I existed as a concept and needed to be represented by something. I had my job clearly out for me from before my existence. I was to facilitate trade, among other responsibilities that eventually arose from my existence. Interestingly, and quite ironically, I do not feel the weight of responsibility like you will normally expect. I do not move around as if carrying the burden placed on me by humans, who existed before me and had huge demands of me even before I came into being.

Many do not know what to do to attract me into their lives. They know they need to interact with me better as they live their lives. However, attracting or retaining me for longer, when they eventually or momentarily come in contact with me, seems to be the huge challenge here.

Some hold tenaciously on to me to their own detriment. They do not realize that they must release me to some extent in order to have more of me. Who wants to be in an abusive relationship – where your stay is not pleasurable, yet your movement outside that space is restricted? Think about it: would you like to be imprisoned?

I see many pray fervently to have me visit them. They envy those who have my attention and believe these people must be manipulating me through some diabolical means, for them to always have me around them. Still, others don't really want to have too much of me around. They love me from afar – at least, that is what they say to themselves and to the world. However, they fear losing control of their lives, if they allow me too much into their space. These people are convinced they will become proud, greedy, self-conceited, etc., if they have me too much of me around them. So, they just wave at me from time to time, as I pass them on my way to the dwellings of those who have learnt how best to interact with me.

You know…

Sometimes, I wonder whether things will be different if there were an age-restriction on interactions with me. Like, you had to wait until age 16 to own a license and drive a car; or go through Aviation School and log in a number of flying hours before you are allowed to fly a plane…you know…something like that.

Maybe people will respect me more. Maybe my relationship with a lot of people will improve considerably. Maybe I will get to spend the night in the dwelling of people I'd love to visit with, rather than be hurried along when I manage to make an entry into their lives. You may be shocked to know that I really want to spend more time with people. I know that I possess great power and hence, can achieve a lot of things within a short time. Yet, I am very malleable. If you acquire the expertise, you can connect with my power and convert me into many more uses than you could ever imagine. Don't worry, I promise to act surprised when you show the world what you have achieved by treating me differently. Lol.

I really want to bring people a measure of liberty. I want people to live free of encumbrances. I want people to live in peace and unity. I want them to live better quality lives than they are currently are living. It will be my joy to see people aspire to more than they ever thought possible. You can say I want them to have better quality 'problems' than what to eat and who borrowed their personal effects. Really, I do!

However, I am very faithful. Because I see others engaging me appropriately, it will be unfaithful (call it dishonest) of me to have put out a blueprint of interactions with me, yet abide with everyone equally.

I would be unfair. I will cause chaos rather than bring peace to the world. I will constantly be mistreated and soon no one will have need of me. I will become so available and therefore not really in high demand. What was that thing you learnt about Demand and Supply in Economics? To a great extent, it is the scarcity of me that gives me value.

So, consider yourself blessed to have come across my autobiography. You will learn a few things about me that will set you apart from people scrambling for pieces of me. In advance, I say Congratulations!

CHAPTER
TWO

I Am Not...

A s I proceed to help you to understand the entity that I am, let us begin by defining who (or what) I am not. Now, I realize you have held impressions of me for long enough, you have come to believe them. Some of them are true and others are not. So, I appeal to you to discard all that you know (and believe) and let's start on a fresh note together, alright?

I Am Not Wicked

Okay, almost everyone wants to be liked. Whether they admit it or not, there is that secret longing to be liked, despite commitments and responsibilities that may dictate otherwise. So, I understand if it is difficult to believe when I say I am not wicked. I mean, would I have admitted to being wicked?

No, I won't.

Seriously, though, you need to allow yourself to believe that I am not wicked. Yes, wicked people have handled me in the past, coloring your opinion of me. Because I could not speak for myself then (you hadn't bought this book, had you?) many got away with labeling me as wicked.

Well, let me state for the records: It is the wickedness already in the heart of my host that comes to light after he suddenly stumbles upon large sums of me.

Sometimes, I wonder who gave them access to my life. Yes, they achieve a lot by my presence in their domain; but the wickedness they did not deal with prior to hosting me comes forth and colors all their accomplishments, making others who are yet to host me to disdain me.

Now you know the truth, though. I am not wicked. I am only powerful enough to reveal the content of the heart of my host.

I Do Not Make People Proud

Your mind may be saying to you that I am simply whining. Believe me; I am not just trying to curry favour from you. Rather, my aim is to give you a new perspective of me to guide our interactions going forward.

Like I said earlier, I reveal the contents of the hearts of people who host me, however temporarily. So when I come in contact with a person, I show to the world that this person is apparently not as humble as he, all the while, pretended to be.

I am not the reason a person is proud or not. A proud person is proud whether he has possession of me or not. One definition of (negative) pride is "a feeling that one is better or more important than other people".

Haven't you come across proud beggars? They insist you must engage with them a certain way even though they need something from you. Pride is an inflated sense of self-worth, often assuming others are not as important as you are. This certainly does not describe my thoughts towards humans. So, please, do not go about hating me, secretly or in the open, because a few people you know who handled me in the past were proud people. In fact, you should thank me for revealing to you who they really are.

I Am Not Evil

There I go again doing all I can to improve your impression of me, yeah? No secret; I'd love it when I achieve that! I would love for you to know me enough NOT to give me absolute power over the circumstances of your life. Remember, absolute power corrupts absolutely! I want you to value fellow humans above me. It is those who run after me, even to the detriment of those around them and humanity in general that subtly fuel the erroneous description of me as "the root of all evil". How painful and untrue!

It is not me who is evil. It is the decision to love me above all else that is evil. So, think about it again. Can you really say I am evil? Or, is it the decision of few people to love me more than they love you that's fueling your thought towards me?

I Cannot Solve All Problems

Did that scare you? No, don't let the truth scare you. I really can't solve all problems. I am not God, am I?
Only God can solve all your problems. So, if you've got a deficiency in your character , acquiring more of me will not solve (or even hide) the problem.

I cannot promise you happiness. And I cannot make you more confident if you are not. I cannot heal all sickness and I cannot give you peace if you are troubled. Hence, even if you manage to camouflage all these deficiencies when the world is watching, you and I know the truth.

We know that there are other ways God can lead you towards solving these problems. And you had better embrace those instructions. Because, even if you borrow some strength from my presence in your life, what happens when I am instructed to step away from you for a bit?

Oh, yes! There are universal principles guiding my engagement with humans. I am under the authority of those principles – under compulsion to obey them.

I Cannot Be Restricted

Too many people think they can restrict my presence to certain locations. They attempt to place me in a mould they have created, ignorant of the fact that I have a clear assignment. I know what I am here to achieve and started work on the day I was born.

No doubt, I am not Omnipresent – I cannot be everywhere I choose to be at the same time (that will reduce the demand for me remember?) My powers are limited to being everywhere I am properly engaged. Only God is Omnipresent, since there are no limits to His powers.

In essence, there are laws guiding my availability and accessibility and one of such laws prohibits my being hoarded.

So, quit believing you will have more of me compared to others by holding me under your mattress, in your bank account, or in some tax haven. You must realize that there are laws regarding engaging me that is no respecter of persons. Engage me properly and I will advance in your direction. That way, you don't have a few people partially amassing me and storing me away, when others have need of me.

Learn to engage with me properly and I will reveal more of myself to you. I will spend more time with you and reveal more of your (good) attributes to the world.

Speaking of attributes....

CHAPTER
THREE

CHAPTER THREE

My Attributes

I wonder if at this stage you are already having a hard time describing me in one word. I agree that will be difficult.

Because first, you need to decide whether I have emotions like every other animate object or not and what these emotions are. Then the next dilemma will be around how to manage my emotions. If, for example, you have believed me to be a WHAT rather than a WHO, then you have to find out what that 'what' is and go on to determine in what form I exist; and possibly, how to collect me and convert me into another form that is more useful and beneficial to you than my current state.

I'll save you all that trouble and just tell you my attributes:

I Am Relative

I am not a lot or not enough on my own. I always need a reference point. If you understand this, you won't waste me; neither will you envy any of my hosts. How do I mean? Have you observed how some people are careless with bits of me in their possession and then go on to wonder why others spend a measure of me on something they consider not worthy of being done with me? You must have people around you who believe that 'rich people' are wasting me in the acquisition of irrelevant things. They say things like, "how can someone in his right frame of mind spend up to $500 on mere laundry in one month?"

It's interesting to note that the same people who make such statements lose bits of me daily to their unchecked cravings. They purchase the things they do not need to impress people who do not know or like them. Sometimes, they turn out to be more wasteful than these people they erroneously judge.

I am relative. I am never spent too much or too little across board. Whether you have engaged me rightly in a particular situation is dependent on you and not the situation. Hence, a measure of me used to procure a particular thing or experience is not too much or too little. The question to answer is: Who are you and what can you really afford?

So, looking at our '$500 on mere laundry' example, one should ask instead: What percentage of this person's disposable income does $500 represent?

I Am Representative

You need to come to terms with that. I am only representative of value. In whatever physical form your country has decided to hold me (including all its variants), I only represent value that can be exchanged.
So, take your mind off the limitation placed by your country and allow yourself to think of me in terms of what people (within and outside your country) are willing to pay for something you are, have or can do.

I represent value. It is what I came to do at the time I was born and it is what I still do today. The implication of this is that, I only visit you based on the value you have – and the perception other people have about that value. If enough people knew about the value in your possession and desire it strongly enough, they will give me your address. It's really that simple.

Quit praying for me without working hard to create value that other people want to pay for. Quit wishing for my visit. If I happen to visit, it will be temporary. Be willing to constantly 'get your hands dirty' and the frequency of my visit to your domain will increase.

I Flow

Okay, I gave you a hint about this when I told you in the last chapter that I cannot be restricted. And now I will expound more on this attribute.

Think of a substance in its liquid state. You know how such a substance flows from one location to another when allowed to move unhindered? Well, I am not a liquid in the sense that you understand a liquid to be, but I flow.

When engaged properly, I flow more in that direction. In a sense, you can say I move around seeking who to dwell with. That is why those who try to hoard me suddenly wake up to realize that they do not have as much of me as they thought relative to those around them.

I Need Structure

I really hope you don't go away thinking I am a liquid but, I have to use that same dimension of me to explain my need for structure.

Think of water collected in a bowl. It can provide you an avenue to wash your hands before or after a meal, at best. Its uses are quite unique and different from water flowing through a tap. Water in this form will very likely be preferable when you need to achieve more than mere washing of hands – for example, to wash your fruits and vegetables before preparation.

Water in the rivers and streams provide you an opportunity to wash clothes in a typical village or irrigate farm lands. But, channeled through massive pipes, the same water becomes even more useful. It can provide water directly to homes and serve entire cities.

Now, let's extend our imagination further to water in a dam. You know how a structure is built to restrict the flow of water until it builds up to a certain height? Great! The water in the dam can then help to drive turbines and generate electricity, useful to an even larger number of people for individual and industrial purposes.

That precisely is my point! I need structure for the impact of my presence to be maximized. So, create a structure for me based on what your end goal is in your interactions with me and I will achieve even more, for you and others around you.

Be individualistic in your choice of structure. Do not fall for the temptation to create your structure according to what other people around you may be building. You can own the island, rather than merely be empowered to visit it once in a while. So, settle down with yourself. Decide on your end goal and then emerge with the appropriate structure for achieving the goal. If you have seen nothing like the structure in your mind's eye before, be bold enough to create it.

Yes, you can! Because...

I Exist First in the Mind

If you think you can host me, you're damn right you can. And if you think you cannot, let me surprise you: You're equally right!

I exist first in the realms of your own possibility. I come around you (a.k.a flow in your direction) based on how much you think is possible within a time frame.

22

What this means is that you need to develop the capacity to believe that we can be friends in large measure. If you don't believe this, I will only reveal a portion of myself to you and keep my visit short. This is why many who win the lottery end up declaring bankruptcy within 5 years of hosting me. Clearly a number of people gave me their address and I visited on schedule. But the lottery winners had not learnt to treat me well, so I flowed in the direction of those who had developed the capacity to host me for long periods.

Create pictorial representations of what you can achieve through me. When a cut-off mark for a level is logged, I get the alert and flow in your direction.

CHAPTER
FOUR

CHAPTER FOUR

How To Engage With Me...

I can tell that by now you are already very restless. I sense that with what you have learnt about me thus far, you are almost bursting with excitement at engaging with me better than you had in the past.

I am excited at re-introducing myself to you, too, and will help you with even more information to help you engage me appropriately. Yes, I am nice like that. Lol.

Create Value

I represent value, remember? So continually create value and you will have me dwell with you perpetually.

No, I did not tell you this earlier, but I sometimes camouflage as problems. The interesting thing is that the same challenges you face, others around you face. So, give yourself to solving problems confronting you and others and you will be creating value that everyone can benefit from. Think of those things you are not satisfied with around you and find a way to create solutions. As you do this, I begin to get signals that it is time to move in your direction.

Remember my account of my birth at the beginning of this my autobiography? Anyone who shows up empty-handed in the market place had nothing to exchange for other people's products, hence he returned home without the products he desired and certainly without me.

Do not be the not-so-smart person described here. Create value. Give people reasons to send me your address and I will come spend time with you.

Stop believing that I am scarce. No I am not! I am everywhere around you, waiting for you to log your demands on my time. When your account hits the cut-off, I will show up at your door step.

Refine Value

If you get stuck thinking 'there is nothing new under the sun', then consider improving on existing solutions. Think: How can I make an existing solution simpler? Faster? Cheaper? Richer? Stronger? Easier to access?

Devote a huge chunk of your time to this thinking exercise and do it often, too. Almost everything can be improved upon. Don't be cowed by the novelty of the idea. That your refined solution does not exist or is not popular yet is not an indication that it won't be embraced. You believe in your idea first, and others will believe in it eventually.

The goods and services you enjoy today represent the limits of one person's effort at thinking. Push further. Allow yourself to dream of the possibilities of an improved solution. It has to happen first in the mind before it becomes tangible.

And when the value you create by refining existing value becomes tangible, when a section of humanity gives me your precise GPS location, I will come in and spend time with you.

Bill for Value

This is one part a lot of people miss it out on, despite their desire that I dwell with them. I mean, they want a measure of me and have earned the right to my presence, too. Make no mistake about that.

Yet, after going through the rigorous thinking process and in many cases, committing physical and emotional resources to the creation of a particular good or service, they go on to give it away for cheap or for free.

Let me point out here that there is a giving dimension to me and I will share this with you in a bit. However you need to be sure you really afford what you are giving out.

Are you refusing to be paid because you are afraid to ask? Is it because you don't know how to charge for your services? Are you finding it difficult to quantify your input? Or, are you ashamed? Could it be you do not want to be seen as 'poor' or beggarly? Do you refrain from asking to be paid because of a past favour?

All the scenarios described above point to the fact that you do not value me as much as you thought you did. It's time to make adjustments in your approach to business. Monetize your input on projects and processes. Then, ask to be paid and set up a system that makes it easy to receive payments, too.

Track Your Expenses

You must keep a log of my visits. Yes, I am that accountable to you. I should not just stroll in and out of your house at will. Make me accountable. Ensure that you are prepared to host me when I come. For how long will you allow me to keep happening on you without telling you in advance?

Track your expenses. Keep a record of where your financial resources are being channeled. It's the first step on your journey to financial freedom. If you will ever be able to create a budget that's reasonable and workable, you have to first keep a record of how I have been deployed in the past.

Get a journal; use an app. Use a spread sheet, whatever works. But you must keep a record of my entry into and exit of your space. Keep at this until it becomes an addiction. That's a safe/highly beneficial addiction to have. Isn't it?

Have A Budget

The age-long advise, yeah? It's age-long because it has worked through the years. If having a budget is no longer relevant, maybe you will be the one to create an alternative. (Remember to bill for your solution, too!)

The gist here is: You must have a budget. Remember I need structure? Your budget is that structure I need, if I will achieve the things you want me to achieve during my stay in your domain. A person's budget shows you what his end-goals are. Sometimes, it is the process of creating a budget that jolts you to reality and forces you to confront your real priorities, irrespective of what you profess.

It is important that I point out here that a budget is composed of two parts. Sadly, many miss out on this crucial fact. Your budget should contain your expected income.

As you plan to send me on errands, you should balance the structure with what you are going to do to earn more of me. Of what use is a car without fuel in it?

Be Deliberate About Your Networks

Remember what I told you about myself in the previous chapter? Do you remember I said that I exist first in the mind? Good. Since you know that, you must choose carefully who is telling you about me consistently. Ensure that you only listen to people who know how to attract and host me for long periods.

If most of the people around you are only giving second-hand information about me, you will soon end up like they are (or even worse). You have the right to choose your friends, so exercise your right. Hang around those who have world-recognized awards as a result of their interactions with me.

You know, of course, that you don't need to meet them in person before you learn from them. Read their articles, buy their books, attend conferences and seminars they speak at, etc. What is really important is not your physical connection with them but access to their minds.

Engage the Supernatural/Value Ideas

No matter what your religious inclination is today, you must agree that I am only relevant while on earth. Once a person dies he has no need for me anymore.

So ensure that you maximize me – exploiting all opportunities that exist in me – while you are alive.

That said, it might interest you to know that I existed in the heavenly realms long before I was born on the earth. While there, I existed in the form of ideas. The same is true of me even today. If you will have me visit your dwelling place in large measures, therefore, you must value ideas.

This is what I referred to when I spoke to you about creating and refining value. I was speaking about ideas – receiving and developing ideas into forms that humans can relate with.

Ideas may come to you in a flash. That is why you must find a way to hold on to them before they fly off again. Keep a notebook close to you – whether it be an electronic or physical notebook. Ensure you always have a means of capturing ideas that come to you, pending when you will develop these ideas.

God is the ruler of both the heavens and the earth. If He will send you the ideas that will empower you to attract me, you must make friends with Him (don't worry, I will show you how at the end of this book). Now, initiating contact with God is the first place to start, but you must also spend time with Him, too, to become His friend.

God loves to gist; He wants to release ideas that will benefit humanity and attract large sums of me to you in the process. He wants to reason with you and teach you how to go about processing or refining ideas that He will drop in your heart.

But He won't intrude in your space. He will keep a respectable distance, except you always invite Him into your affairs.

The Giving Dimension

I remember hinting you earlier that there is a giving dimension to me. You see, aside solving problems for people, another way to attract me is to give. I know this sounds contradictory, so let me help you understand what I am saying.

Ordinarily, when you take a thing out of a pool, the quantity of what you have in the pool reduces. However, though I exist in the world, my original citizenship is of heaven. So just like any ambassador in a country, my activities and manifestations are governed by the laws of my home country.

In my home country, your supply is in your giving and not in your receiving alone. When you give, you register your power over greed. You communicate with me that you have put me in my rightful position – I am NOT more important to you more than your fellow humans. When I get this message, I flow more in your direction. Do you know why?

It's because I want to establish the kingdom of God on earth! I do not want to be used to contravene any law in my home country. I prefer to dwell with those who will co-operate with God to bring peace and ease to the people He dearly loves.

Will you join me on this assignment?

CHAPTER
FIVE

CHAPTER FIVE

Now that you know

This has been the most vulnerable me thus far! I doubt I have ever held such a conversation with anybody. Thank you for allowing me to be this open with you.

Well...

Now that you know all that you have learnt about me in this book, where do we go from here? And, how do we interact going forward?

Let me share a few things you may add to the decisions you have already made.

Know Your Net Worth

Make a list of all you own and all you owe. Write down and put figures to all that bears your name and can be sold. Ensure the figure you put down is not what you paid for those possessions, but what you will be paid if you had to dispose of them urgently. Add all these figures up and let's call this Figure 1.

Next, make a list of all you need to pay. Remember to include payments that will fall due in future and ensure that the figure you write down is the future value you have to pay for what you owe today. Do an addition of all on this list; let's call this Figure 2.

Now, subtract Figure 2 (the total from your second list) from Figure 1 (the total from your first list). What you get is your net worth. Don't fret if this figure is in the negative. We'll talk about how to get it positive in a bit. And if your net worth is positive, don't retire yet.

Pay Off Your Debts

Take a look at your second list from the Net-worth Calculation exercise above. Can you rank the contents of this list according to some criterion of your choice? You may number them according to amount owed, interest paid on each, financial and emotional implications for delayed repayment, etc. Whichever the criterion you choose to adopt for the classification of outstanding debts, you are in the right. This is because your choice will be made based on your peculiar circumstances. No one criterion is more important than the other.

Now, you should go on to pay off your debts, one debt package at a time. Earmark a certain percentage of your earnings to debts repayments. No matter how little this percentage comes to, as long as you remain consistent, you will pay off your debts in a shorter time than you thought possible.

There are so many benefits of doing this. It frees you up to take advantage of opportunities that come up in the course of living your life. It also helps you to believe in possibilities and take the (calculated) risks you must take to attract me to your dwelling.

As you begin to pay off your debts, choose your motivation. You may display how much you have paid off thus far or how much is left before you are done paying off that particular debt package. Whatever gives you the greater motivation to keep sacrificing, go ahead and adopt this. Display the figures in strategic locations around you – on your phone, on a board in your bedroom, dining area, office, etc.

You are working hard at getting your life in order again. Everything you own should contribute to providing you the continued encouragement you need to follow-through with your debt-repayment commitment. And, these are cost-free ways to obtain motivation, so why not use them?

Build an Emergency Fund

When you are done paying off your debts (and you can do this alongside paying off your debts, too), the next thing to do is to build an emergency fund.

An Emergency Fund is a pool of funds that covers your expenses for up to 3 months, if you suddenly stop earning an income. Better if you can make it up to 6 months' expenses, but 3 months is a good enough benchmark.

It is after you have paid off your debts and built your emergency fund that you will proceed to investing your income – making it work for you even harder than you worked for it.

Create a Bucket List

A bucket list is a list that contains all you want to achieve, own or experience before you kick the bucket. It reveals to you (and everyone you share it with) what is really important to you. Your bucket list reminds you of all you must achieve while here on earth. It can help you overcome greed (as described above). It encourages you to delay gratification and pay the price now for the future you want for yourself and for those you are concerned about.

So, take some time out. Get comfortable with a glass of water or your favorite drink, close your eyes for a few minutes and allow your mind to wander.

Think of your funeral. What would you like said about you by the people closest to you? What solutions will you like to bring to the world? What is that situation you suffered and would like to ensure no one else does? What is that place you will like to vacation at? Or, that place you'd like own? Who is that person you would like to be?

Take away all the constraints you might come across, as you perform this exercise. For a moment, imagine the world is a perfect place and that you already have all the resources that you need to actualize all the dreams contained in your heart. Write down all that comes to mind and there you have your bucket list!

As you did in the case of debt repayments, keep your bucket list in view. Paste it on your vision board. It will register in your mind what you desire to enjoy or experience. And, that's where you'll find the inner strength to keep making the sacrifices that must be made for your dreams to come true.

Start Investing Early

There are only so many hours you can work for. With everyone having a limit of 24 hours a day and with physical strength (ordinarily) diminishing as you age, it is wisdom to maximize your youth.

Start investing early. Let compound interest work for you. Don't fret if you feel like you should have started investing earlier than now and you didn't. Better to start tomorrow than the day after; even better to start today than tomorrow.

Use your bucket list as a guide to determine how much you will need to fulfill all those dreams of yours. Then create a plan that will ensure their fulfillment, as much as lies with you.

Too many people are unconsciously setting themselves up to never be able to truly retire. Without giving it much thought, or any thought at all, the way they live their lives today predict that they will be forced to work for as long as they are alive. Do not join that statistic. By virtue of this conversation we've had, it will be my joy to see you retire when you want to retire and not a day later.

Value Time

As mentioned during our discussion on investing, if you will have me visit you for an extended period of time – if you need my help ticking off the items you have on your bucket list – you must value time.

Have you considered carefully the fact that the richest and poorest people on earth each have access to the same number of hours per day? God is that fair – everyone has access to the same 24 hours. The difference in net-worth and economic well-being from one person to another is in the value of 1 hour of their time.

You recall I told you to strive to increase your net-worth every year? One place to focus your attention on, if you will do this, is in the use of your time. How much is 1 hour of your time worth today? And, how much do you want it to be worth 2 years from today?

Create a detailed plan of how you will use your time now to achieve all that is on your bucket list. Some people call this exercise goal setting. I'm not sure what you call it, but I know that valuing time is one way to ensure you do not live the same year 120 times and call it a lifetime.

Thank you for your time, my dear friend. It's been great spending the last few hours, days, weeks (hey, how long did it take you to read this book, anyway?) with you.

As We Round Off Our Conversation...

I promised to let you know how you can make friends with God so as to spend time with Him and ensure a constant flow of 'ideas' in your direction.

There are two basic steps to friendship with God:

1.   Believe in His Son, Jesus Christ.
2.   Confess your belief.

Here…

Take a look at the following Scripture…

•It's the word of faith that welcomes God to go to work and set things right for us. This is the core of our preaching. Say the welcoming word to God—"Jesus is my Master"—embracing, body and soul, God's work of doing in us what he did in raising Jesus from the dead. That's it. You're not "doing" anything; you're simply calling out to God, trusting him to do it for you. That's salvation. With your whole being you embrace God setting things right, and then you say it, right out loud: "God has set everything right between him and me!"

(Romans Chapter 10 Verses 9 – 10 MSG)

Therefore, say the following prayer:

"Dear God, I believe that Your Son, Jesus Christ, died for my sins on Calvary's cross.
I confess my sin and accept you into my life as my personal Lord and Savior. Thank you for saving me. In Jesus' Name I pray. (Amen)"

Because Olubunmi Samuel-Adeyemi facilitated our discussion today, I invite you to send her an e-mail at olubunmi@limerglobal.com and have her guide you in your new friendship with God.

I have thoroughly enjoyed spending time with you and hope you feel empowered more than ever before to interact profitably with me. There are a number of people around the world living life on their own terms. This day, I welcome you to the club.

Congratulations!!!

About LIMER Personal Finance

LIMER Personal Finance is a Personal Finance practice providing Money Therapy and Financial Literacy services to African business owners.

At **LIMER** Personal Finance, we believe that since everyone interacts with money, education about money is a right that everyone should have.

This is why we have created and deployed training programmes for teenagers, undergraduates, job-seekers, business and career professionals and market women.

Please visit www.limerglobal.com to learn more about our work, including impact made since we commenced operations.

Join our mailing list here:(www.limerglobal.com/connect   ).

About the Book

Ever imagined what a conversation with Money will look like? What will Money say to you about it and how to engage with it? Should Money even be referred to as an 'it'? Is Money instead human? Does Money have a gender, a race or other ethnic, political or socio-economic affiliations? Or, is Money a spirit like you have heard for so long? Does it have a mind of its own? And, does it have a mind at all?

These and many more are the questions answered in Hello! My Name Is Money. It is an autobiography of Money with no mention of the word "Money". In it, Money shares for the first time who/what it is, is not, how to engage appropriately with it and even invites you to

About the Author

Olubunmi Samuel-Adeyemi is a Money Therapist at LIMER Personal Finance (www.limerglobal.com). She is constantly conducting Money Therapy sessions for individuals and families to confront their money problems and find lasting solutions to them.

Her mission is to inspire people to greater achievements by helping people tidy up their finances so that they can live life on their own terms; rather than be confined to socio-economic levels and systems they are not happy about. This she does via individual and specialized group training programs for teens, youths, business and career professionals and market women. Her very insightful articles have also been read all around the world.

Acknowledgements

The manuscript for this book was written on May 14 and 15, 2016. The idea was burning, power supply to type it up was non-existent, so I wrote it by hand.

Thank You, Lord, for how You orchestrated my path all those years, bringing me into experiences that make this book a rich one.
The Stallion – my king, my husband – Samuel Oluwaseun Adeyemi. Thank you, Oba, for being selfless in your love for me. Particularly on this book project, thank you for leading the way.

Oluwaseun, Olayinka, Omotola, IfeOluwa and Tomiwa Fawunmi comprise the best family a person could ever belong to. With them, you are sure your love bank could never be empty. Thank you, for accepting me as a worthy addition to the bunch.

Yetunde Macaulay graciously invited Olawale Adedotun Olosunde to type up this manuscript when it mattered the most. Thank you, Dotun, for doing this sacrificially and meticulously. And, thank you, Youthful Yetunde, for being my co-labourer in development and for the many ways in which you support projects I am involved in.

Olushola "Solarspeaks" Adigun was one good thing that came out of the meeting in Abuja. I enjoyed the many brainstorming sessions we had before emerging with the book cover, Olushola. Thank you for being so gifted, yet so patient.

I run to Nadu Denloye with questions about everything. Thank you, Dr. D., for being a person I can trust with both my personal and my professional life. Every time I think of you, I acknowledge that God answered my prayers to send me to serve His child.

Kehinde Adetiloye is a rare one. Super-talented yet hardworking, relational yet thorough, he continues to egg me on to greater and deeper learning. Thank you, Dr. Adetiloye, for making Finance attractive, for the clarity you provide at every point and for your commitment to ensuring I "balance it well".

After I had carried a vision for almost 4 years, it was such a joy to discover that Peter Mbama was already living it. Mr. Mbama, you have helped me to expand my vision of inspiring people to greater achievements. Thank you for your belief in me, for investments made in my thinking and for the respect you have for me. I am truly grateful.

My friends, business associates and participants at LIMER Personal Finance programs helped to clarify some of the concepts presented in this book and situate these concepts in the 21st century. Thank you for the interactions, thought-provoking questions and continued support.

Thank you!

www.ingramcontent.com/pod-product-compliance
Lightning Source LLC
Chambersburg PA
CBHW041715200326
41519CB00001B/174